Bright Skies, Long Shadows

An Anthology

Marcus Turner

First published in 2023.

Copyright © Marcus Turner 2023

Marcus Turner has asserted his right to be identified as the author of this work in accordance with the Copyright, Designs and Patents Act 1988

ISBN: 9780645882612

All rights reserved. No part of this publication may be reproduced, stored in a retrieval system, or transmitted, in any form or by any means, electronic, mechanical, photocopying, recording or otherwise, without the express prior permission of the author/publisher.

Cover design by Marcus Turner

streamofmadness.wordpress.com.au

Dedication

This book is dedicated to my children, without whom my days would not be so bright, and my shadows that much longer.

Portrait

I see my reflection
>> distorted

At angles in the train window.

Two mouths where my eyes should be
>> And clumps of hair clogging my ears.

I am blind and deaf
>> Yet ever the speaker.

Sometimes I think this is a
>> Very accurate portrait.

Wallflower

i am lost in the crowd
       invisible
a shadow unseen
   by the caster
brick fading among
       exhaled smoke
paint decaying on apathetic walls
   wallflower supreme
   scribing ghosts and phantasms
       unseen
as the world wheels and laughs around me.

Hell Redefined (Hell I)

      is hell truly a cauldron of fire
  for the souls of the damned
      the concentric nightmare
          Virgil
          shewed to Dante?

there is no fire and brimstone in this hell I know.

fingers of ice and frost cling to the walls
              of a world
      sharing the same sun, yet
      whose brilliant light filters blue
          through the gloom
          of an overlapping sky.

a hell not found in holy books

or pseudopolitical metaphor,

but a hell right here on loamy earth,

        beneath my shuffling feet.

a hell seen even through eyes

        misted by cold smoke

        fixed on worldly hungers

        perceived even by a mind

        inoculated against its pain.

a winter prolonged by choice

        vice

        mannish folly.

the permanent season of my discontent.

        a wonderland is filled

            with fun rides

and diversions

and delirious camaraderie

yet a price of admission

beyond my ability

or willingness

to pay.

are there harriers in this

obscenely familiar abyss?

angels of the fall

in this hell of mine?

oh yes, there are demons—

torturers forged by our very own hands:

that such nightmares could be fashioned

from agony

and simple,

fragile

glass.

slender of body and bulbous of head,
with no extremities to call its own,
yet somehow the demon still travels
        with me through this hell
                as my sole companion—
                my rod, my whip.
a face expressionless, yet it has a mouth
        and inside an icy tongue
      by which I am both beckoned
                and condemned.

this hell of mine, this shaded parallel world
 in which my agony has taken new root;
a glacial prison from which I cannot escape
unless—

unless I am brave, and

appeal before the demon

who holds my soul hostage

    in this hell.

are the devils we know so much better?

    why fight when submission

        frees the mind

        cuts the pain

    from all places it is found?

    NO

        i am dying

yet how much comfort

    the warm, safe oblivion

        i've felt in its embrace.

waiting

    lingering

                    uncertain of what to do

i grapple with the fiend of glass
        wrestling like jacob against god
        and
        against hope
        i overpower the demon
screaming against its poison in my ears
 thrusting it to the ground,
and with a brief shrill scream
its brittle body is sundered
                beyond saving

perhaps to be sent to a hell of its own.

the demon is gone, now
        but years on
my frosty hell remains

if only in spirit

whose ghost will haunt me

for the rest of my days

if only to force remembrance

    of what little

        in hell's

        servitude

    i gained, and

    of all I lost.

The Picture on my Office Wall (Portrait II)

A storm shook the foundations of my house one night—

Or it might have been an earthquake, I don't remember—

It was not a terribly memorable event, I am sure,

But strife need not be apocalyptic in scale

For its effects to be acutely felt.

I recall, albeit passingly, how, miraculously

Only books, a few loose papers toppled and scattered,

And a cherished family photo, came

Crashing

Down from my office wall

That terribly innocuous night.

How many times have I entered that
room since without ever noticing ,
Without comprehending
The destruction wrought by that
unremarkable event?
The shattered frame, the torn glossy
paper,
Shards of glass like crystalline lotuses
Strewn upon a cloudy grey pond—
How long before I realised just how
damaged,
How inconceivably, irreparably distorted
That cherished image was?

Our canvas faces, once smiles,
Contorted into grimaces and glares,
Our embrace divided by crease lines;
Worst damaged is the image of myself,

A jagged shard embedded in my face:
Monstrous, unrecognisable.
Why do we see things as they really are,
Too late?

I bend down to pick up the glass
But my hands are bare, and the pieces are sharp.
Silvery needles lance my fingers,
Jagged shards split my palms
Casting ribbons upon the floor.
I clutch my hand, gasping:
Like pinot noir upon white shag carpet,
It will never be undone,
The blood will never come out.
The compact is broken, my bleeding both payment and reminder:
I have not upheld my end of the bargain.

You see

Families, like glass, are fragile things:

Handle them with care and they are beautiful;

Drop them and they shatter into a thousand knives,

Cutting the mishandled and mishandler alike.

No one gets out alive.

You die in that moment

And for better or worse

Become someone else.

Newborn babes, seeded with bitterness

And born with atrophied hearts,

Diverging down well-trodden paths

Splitting at the yellowed wood.

I give up picking up the glass, nursing

instead

    the damaged photograph,

    Tears splashing against the frozen, smiling faces,

    Stroking them tenderly,

    Smudging them accidentally with a bloody thumb-print.

    I can no longer see them clearly and

    It is my fault.

    My wounded image,

    Divided by a splinter—

    A wound of the psyche as much as of image—

    Abusing, accusing:

    I am broken and this is my fault.

    It is an accusation I cannot weather and

    I must look away.

    But how can I stop this prophecy

If I do not look?

How can the madness of history cease

Repeating itself?

Speak No Lies

Do not ask which creature

Screams in the night

If you do not wish to know

The truth.

Do not ask the flower to open

If you cast upon it the shade.

Do not set out to clear the cobwebs

If unprepared for spiders' bites.

Do not ask me to speak

If all you want is stoic silence

And suffering compressed into

Needlepoints behind the eyes.

Do not ask the dam to open

If you cannot bear the crush of the

Rushing river.

The vampire does not crack his sternum

And bare his bleeding heart

Before the axe

The scythe

And the immolating flame;

He does not emerge from

His nocturnal exile

Embracing the sun

When it reveals its traitor's touch.

So do not ask which creature screams in the night:

You don't really want to know,

And I don't want to lie,

And so it will remain in shadow;

The truth will languish in silence.

Do not lament or chastise

When the fiend emerges

To feed and exsanguinate

And destroys all around him:

You made him a monster when

You robbed him the chance

To be a man.

Heretic

Looming on the horizon

A tower in eclipse,

Blinding white thrusting upwards

Against dying day.

I am no pilgrim,

But a faithless destroyer coming to

Tear down these hollow walls.

Inside, upon crumbling thrones,

The tower's castellans—

How many have fallen by their hand?

How many swayed by honey-dripped words

And empty sweet nothings?

How much blood has been scrubbed clean

From these walls and floors

By prostrate neophytes?

Far more than can be seen.

Death and ruin follows in their dogma's wake.

Merchants in the narthex demand a high price
For a starved goat of the sacrifice.
Me, when I have so little already to give?
But my freedom, someone told me—
Someone who had already taken
Their pound of flesh—
Had been paid for in blood.
Now, you tell me,
It must be purchased again, with gold?

The eaves glitter with gold leaf and
The nave shines resplendent.
Yet none present can see the weeping walls,
The profane acts performed
By non-sacral whores;
Nor familiar-faced satyrs

Cavorting in their secret sin
Upon the temple's stained glass windows,
Nor the cracks spider-webbing
The alabaster altar.
Dilapidation and decay is hidden everywhere
But the throngs are in thrall,
Bent low by the mind-softening drone
Of the demagogue's babbling tone.

Ha! I was once a favoured son in this tower!
But nemesis cleared the fog from my eyes,
Sat upon judgement like a cucking stool
And an icy dunk in the river!
I was blind, and naive—
To think love could heal and redeem
If I ran afoul of the demagogue's esteem!

Now upon your "holy" earth I spit

And I roar to you all in the Tower in defiance—
I will not be condemned
By your self-righteousness
Or your false, hollow piety!
Only to a King no tower can seat
Could I ever pledge my allegiance!

My apostasy, cast with the rabble-rousers,
The sinners and fallen saints—
HERETIC! the chorus sang,
A poisonous dirge seeping down
From shadow-strewn eaves:
HERETIC!
If only your followers,
Those blissful, ignorant
Transfixed sheep,
Knew of the darkness,
The hypocrisy, in you I saw.

If only they saw the blood smeared on their cheeks
From where your hand has blessed them.
They do not realise how alone they truly are,
And that God does not reside here.

Anchors

I am drowning

My hand slipping empty beneath the waves

My lungs filling with water

Black bubbles exploding in my brain.

I cannot think or speak

I can only scream

But I cannot let it out

My lungs filled with concrete.

I fall into the abyss like a stone

A bird falling from the sky

Burial at sea

Spiralling down against hope.

I am cold

The sun cannot reach me where I sink

Everywhere is murk, murk,

I cannot see—

The detritus of the past,

Food for thought and the present
And future,
Cloudy and obfuscating instead
As it sinks into the depths with me.
My passion will die alongside the light.
My lungs, my heart, my thoughts
Drag me down like cement shoes
Laying me to rest in a river that yawns
As wide as the ocean,
Such is the pressure.
I am drowning
And I am the anchor.

Strangers

Slamming doors and glacial chills—
When did we become such strangers?
When did we begin glorifying our spiteful wills,
The sizzling flame of our love waver?

When did we become such strangers,
Our words like cudgels, bloody and slick;
The sizzling flame of our love wavers,
The wall in our home rising brick by brick.

Our words like cudgels, bloody and slick,
Daggers carving slices, infected runnels;
The wall in our home rising brick by brick,
A divide under which we can no longer tunnel.

Daggers carving slices, infected runnels—
Our words are few but savage, silence reigns supreme,
A divide under which we can no longer tunnel.
We've gone as far as we dared yet dream.

Our words are few but savage, silence reigns supreme,
We meet each other's eyes, the knowledge a blister:
We've gone as far as we dared yet dream;
Now the dream dies with but a whisper.

We meet each other's eyes, the knowledge a blister—
When did we begin glorifying our spiteful

wills?

Now the dream dies with but a whisper,

Amid slamming doors and glacial chills.

Head Full of Ghosts

Pain is not sharp—

A clean cut dividing fledgling cells

And generational memory—

It is a sledgehammer

against brittle limbs,

Shattered bones floating

From swollen sausage digits

And bruised, tumescent limbs

Flowing towards the heart.

Voices in the brain,

Tarnished and hoary:

Whispers of the ancients

Like insidious sleeper agents;

The croaking of demons and lechers,

Spiders and wretches,

Men of fists and men of absence.

A head full of ghosts,

Speaking the secret languages of fear.

Memories not mine,

But circumstances across time;

Thirsts and vices loaded before birth

Upon my yawning sapling back.

It didn't start in this place,

But time will not erase—

The end is always on the morrow.

The dying of the light began yesteryear.

I never had a chance.

The road marches ever on,

Ever more pitted by the unceasing rain

And the promise of this inexorable

Incurable curse.

A reminder, yes:

I know where this road leads—

Comforting in the way
Of familiar devils.
But can I divert this road, in time—
For them, for myself?
Is it simply inevitable?
Did I ever have a choice?
Pain isn't sharp or clean
But a slew of broken bones
Floating down the red river of time
Screaming one agonised imperative:
To banish these ghosts from my head,
Lest I soon wind up dead
And spell calamity for the ones
Arriving next.

Letters Home

Dear Nan,

It's been a while, wherever you are
I hope this letter finds you doing good:
It's been so long already,
God, it feels like yesterday;
But time has a way of making yesterday
Feel like eternity and a day.
I miss you more than ever;
The road has been long and lonely.
I suppose I chose this path, one might say,
When I first stepped on that plane.
I had good reason, and I know you
Know it now, probably better than
You did back then.
But loneliness is more than just

How much country stands between us.

My heart is filled with regret—

That the plane, and all those

Long years in between,

Until those final moments in the hospice,

Masquerading as a nursing home;

All that time I spent in hiding,

Languishing in shame,

Shutting out the one ray of light

From that earliest part of my life.

That biting scent of bleach

Barely masking the loamy soil of death,

I got a taste of that lost light,

The glimmer of recognition—

And your sweet, sweet smile—

Before I lost it all over again.

I got to say goodbye,

But I wish we'd had more time.

So much I wanted to tell you,

So much I wanted to explain,

So much forgiveness to seek.

I wanted to thank you,

For protecting me over the years,

For loving me when

Love felt a chore in the giving and receiving;

For all the times you forgave

For all the bad things I did,

All the times you defended me,

Saw my spark

But did not try to snuff it out.

It's the closest to unconditional love

I've ever had.

It didn't strip away my life's sadness,

Nor the trajectory

My life would eventually take,

But I shiver when I think that, without you,

How much worse it all might have been.
When you took me into your arms,
I felt it was safe to cry;
When you held me close,
I no longer wanted to die.
I did not give that love back in kind,
And it tore me apart even all those years
While you were still alive.
I got older, my children were born and
My own life took priority.
While everybody else drew closer,
I drew further away.
Not on purpose—I was just afraid
That you'd not want to talk to me
Or that you'd be ashamed of what
I'd made of my life.
I should have known better—
God I was stupid—

You never ever judged me,

And if even if you did, you kept it

To yourself and never for a moment

Let disapproval eclipse that tenderness.

I'll never forget those final moments

I spent with you—

Despite my dawning horror of the scene,

The palpable closing of the curtain

On a scene of utter tragedy,

The youth, flooding back

Into your cloudy eyes,

Lasting but a few minutes

Amid the bodily pain

And fog of the weary mind;

The moment of candor and

The unspoken totality between us.

In three days you were gone,

But even before then

We knew everything would be all right.
I still beat myself up sometimes, Nan,
When I think about all the lost time,
All the times I could have picked up
The phone, even for ten minutes.
There's no getting that back now,
And that will haunt me for the
Rest of my earthly days.
But sometimes I swear you're still around.
Occasionally I feel a chill,
As if you're visiting, prickling
The air around me;
Sometimes I feel your smiling eyes and
Soft hand, I swear, touch my forearm.
No one is ever really gone,
So long as they're remembered
And cherished.
And so I cherish you:

Wish you were here more every day,
Even when my life is so ugly
I can't bear the thought of
You witnessing.
Well, Nan,
I guess it's time for me to finish this.
If you can hear this, see this,
Feel my heart,
Though my actions might have told
A tale different from the one I wished
Or different from the one I'm telling now,
I am and always was with you,
Just as you were and are with me.
I know I turned away and ran,
But don't ever forget:
I did, do and always will
Love you, Nan.

Mania In Media Res

can't think straight
    just want to light a
        match
and set the whole fucking thing on
        fire
and dance around the ashes and ruin
    until my madness
        abruptly ends
        and my regretful tears
        make ink of the ash
          and soot daubed on my skin.
i am drunk on this
    fever dream
        of abandon and
    self-destruction.
  a brain-pan full of pins
    and needles

      scourging soft pink and grey
    to bloody rags.
all caution cast
    like fiberglass rain
        into the downwind
           i face headlong.
    haha.
i am in danger.

Nepenthe

Sweet oblivion

Open your genie bottle and

Pour down my throat

Strip me away and fill me with

Warm emptiness

Scrub me away until nothing remains.

Wash me away, rinse me clean, my

Teacher, mother,

My secret lover.

Erase me as I

Quaff this glorious nepenthe,

Sharpen my pain so

Pain is all I know,

Brilliant in its eclipsing glare,

A cruel kindness

To give my flight

Blinding, screaming meaning.

Drown me and let me rise

Baptised

Cleansed

Freed from memories

Of what might have been,

Leaving no elegy for

What has been lost.

Pain without memory—

Hallelujah, Amen!—

The sweetest kind.

Rattlesnake venom,

Just a little will do,

But too much is too easy

And so sweet and swift is your

Succor.

Should I stay or should I run?

Should I sojourn or should I

Sleep?

So many questions I cannot answer

As the midnight train carries me to the twilight station;

So much uncertainty I can't

Bear to face

Without you.

Morrigan

Morrigan,

Sweetest darkness,

Have you cast your bones for me?

Sifted through the guts of pigs

Or combed the entrails of the dead

      To measure my worth?

Have your ravens whispered something of note

      In your ear

That stays your pallid hand from tripping

      The trapdoor of my gibbet?

Are you generous unspooling the cord of

      My life,

      Meagre and cruel for others?

Phantom queen, reaper of souls,

Am I unworthy, too, to reap?

      To glean meaning from my threshing?

Or am I mad for decrying
    Such years of oblivious, ignorant
peace,
    Scrabbling for an unhappy lie at best
    And at worst an impossible
abstraction?
    Why have you
Spared me from your embrace when I have
    Courted your doom all these long
years,
If only to perpetuate the weave of suffering?
    To have glimpses of the sun,
    Only to snatch the light

    Away?

The Hell of Self (Hell II)

Contrary to Sartre

Hell isn't other people:

When you look into the self long enough

Hell is the mirror-twin,

The panda-eyed, clammy-skinned

Spectre with an icepick stare,

A master sum of neglect

And pain with roots plumbing so deep

They will never see the sun.

No exit from such naked truth,

Such confusion and despair.

An enigma in the mirror;

Affectations of hallucination,

The sleet of self-doubt

That will thaw on warmer days.

It's easy to deceive others,

But even easier to deceive oneself:

The miraculously functioning machine,

Functioning out of spite for the jury-rigging of its

Ill-fitted parts:

A thousand hopes and dreams

Buoying a life upon boneless spaghetti legs

Through low-hanging mist;

But it cannot maintain the illusion forever:

Those soft, limp appendages will not bear

The weight of such lofty expectations.

That I would be so lucky

Even just to crawl.

Bloodless eyes sink back into fleshy pockets,

Budding flowers wilting with ennui and

fatigue

Until all that remains, within and without, is

Rage and shame—

Hatred and loathing turned inward.

I am exhausted;

Tired of pretending

To know myself,

To love myself,

Of recognising the horror I see in the mirror

Or the smiling mask mounted slipshod upon it.

I'm tired of pretending to understand my needs

Or know how to function as a man

Instead of a broken boy

Nursing scars as freshly gaping wounds

Instead of faded stripes from long dead days.

I'm tired, so tired, of this

Inexorable conceit

Of meaning in this chaos,

Purpose to discern in

The maelstrom's roar—

Ha! All such noise,

Sound and crushing fury,

Signifying nothing but my

Indulgent, whispered conceits.

I am unfinished;

Hope shines upon this reckoning

in my brighter moments,

Offering me a chance.

Yet I am afraid of

What I may instead find:

A medicore artist's misconception,

Michelangelo's David

Only partway realised

Before the artist, restless,

Sets down his chisel and retires—

A wiser man acknowledging a doomed product

Time will not forgive nor redeem.

The question remains: am I the artist

Or the failed work?

Am I the writer

Or the written—

My destiny wax-sealed, the way prepared,

For the future to confirm

The wisdom of the artist's departure?

Do I march onward into the fray—

One damaged, weary man

Against the slithering horde vomiting forth from the abyss

Wearing my face—
Knowing I cannot escape this hell,
Yet wage war against its demons anyway,
Gnashing my teeth, tasting iron,
Roaring my battle-cry in a desperate final stand,
Bearing my axe and rage against the ghosts
Reflected in my broken mirror parts?
Will rage
And blind, stupid, heedless optimism
Be enough
To set me free of the
Hell of myself?

Lamplight Confessions

I can't stand what has become of my life.
I can't stand knowing I'll never be free,
Never be free of you.
The chains, broken, but
The manacles still chafe my wrists.
Pinned, paralysed,
But for my eyes
That play voyeur to my unmanning,
And those of the succubus
Sitting on my chest
Keeping me from sleep.
How far back in time would I go
To undo what has been done?
Would I have returned your affections,
Swooped in to help you correct course
Whereupon you had drifted in

From a cruel and tempestuous sea?
Would I have turned a deaf ear to your whispers of love?
Would I have drawn you into my bed,
Taken you into my confidences?
Would I have even dared
To reach around your hips,
Tilt your head towards mine
For that first intoxicating kiss,
To spare myself from the beauty and pain
In every spawning memory's refrain?
If I could tear through the firmament
And cross the thresholds of time,
How far would I go?
Would I, *could I*, be the nail
Upon which our history would unravel,
Dissolving into errant threads
That would never singularly converge?

I would be no wiser,

And there are many blessings I cannot undo

Despite everything they have cost.

But I would not know this pain, this dull ache

That persists long after the tapestry's weaving has

Ceased,

The thousand leaking cuts that will not heal,

The trust I cannot bring back from the dead,

Not even for myself.

If I could tear through the firmament

And cross the thresholds of time,

I confess—

I would not have been, nor shall I be

again,
    Someone's lukewarm soup

    To be reheated

    When the winter's pickings are meagre;

    I would not have been, nor shall I be

again,

    A harbour for the lost

    Desperately chasing safety

    Limping battered and broken

    After such violent and cruel storms.

    I have my own mercurial weathers to face

    And the cove, that was once my heart,

    Has finally closed,

    Possibly forever.

    I doubt it will open.

Melancholia

When the meds
    Aren't working
And the *oms* aren't resonating
    And all the creativity
        In the world cannot
            Exorcise the demonic
            Rage or hideous ennui
                Of the moment;
When the slow trudge of the day
        Dries up all the water
           A man has to live,
And his midnight fire
        Has dipped to its lowest ebb,
What is there to do?
How can a man fight through
    The sludge sucking at his heels

And make it out alive?

Aries + Virgo

Be the fire to my earth:
    Fire incites,
        Earth placates.
Can you ground me, you ask?
    Can you show me the beauty in simple things?
Yes, I answer, with a counter:
    Can you rejuvenate the soil?
        Can you heal my broken wings?
Don't treat me gently—
        Love me hard and fierce.
Would that I have loved so intensely,
    So recklessly,
        A sizzling caress
    That leaves a puckered mark of its
    Passing.

To remember the transience of passion
    And fathom its rare magnificence;
To remember that it will come and go
    And then come again.
Don't argue with me that there's
    no tenderness
        In the destructive heat:
The earth needs to be scorched,
    now and then,
For new and beautiful things to grow again.
    Who is to say the land cannot thrive
    in the presence of
    all-consuming flame?
Don't treat me gently:
    I don't want it and
        My heart can take it.
I've withstood that much and worse,
    All to light but a brief candle

In this

Endless sea of night.

Elysium

Beacon, lighthouse,

Sun and moon,

The path is lit because of you.

An echo of love lost

Though your memory be innocent—

Pure and sweet like spring water.

Anchor to the earth but

Piece of the divine, too—

An angel who saved a

Life not worth saving.

Your love has carried me

Broken on a litter,

Dried my tears and

Forced me to my feet

In the face of snarling defeat;

Pierced the bedrock

Around my heart

And turned impregnable stone into

Beating flesh once more.

Little one,

My sins cannot be washed away

But still I walk away cleaner,

Standing a little taller,

Knowing I had a hand

In one good thing

That can never be undone.

You are my proof:

In the collision of chaotic probability,

In the tumult of sequencing

And uncooperative cells

Perfection can arise.

Flesh of my flesh,

Blood of my blood—

Wherever you go,

I will always be with you.

You are my greatest creation,

My wisest teacher,

My most faithful companion

On this lonely road.

I know that between

Cradle and grave

I will walk with you,

As you walk with me.

I will throw you into the sky

To strengthen your fledgling wings

And catch you when you fall.

And when the time is right,

I will set you out to flight.

Beacon, lighthouse,

Golden sun to my silver moon.

My path is lit because of you.

The Long Night

Sitting upon a roughhewn log,

Bathed in roaring firelight

I gaze across the darkened valley

Up at the silvery pinpricks

Wheeling in black velvet above.

Hands outstretched towards the fire,

I pull them back, for fear of burning,

Warm,

Smiling and laughing,

Before I realise how long I've sitting alone

afore that mountain fire.

The fire's glow ebbs away,

The valley creeping closer,

Cold indifferent nature smothering the warmth

Bringing with it the defeat inherent
Imminent
Of coals, ashes.

The great alpine tapestry darkens,
A bas relief against the remaining light.
I am alone on this mountain but yet there is an enemy in that darkness—
How long before the light fades and I am left
Shivering in that darkness,
Unable to see myself
Unable to recall the ghost of who I was?

The valley approaches,
Beckoning but not with the voice of crisp gales
Stroking arm-hairs to erection

But with the empathy of the broken:

"Come with me—

"Lose yourself in me.

"Walk into the valley and

"Don't look back.

"The fire is hot and burns,

"Burning all it touches.

"It does not love you.

"Not as I love you.

"Life gives me gifts

"And I keep them forever.

"Be with me—

"You won't be alone, here in the darkness.

"Do not mourn or despair

"The fire's dying light.

"Life's light burns,

I am its salve, its mercy."

The firepit is cold now,

The great forest so dark

Not even the moon can light it.

Only at the centre - the place where coals

Still glow defiant—

Does the fire remain seeded.

The long night weighs heavily upon my back and

I almost reach to touch the valley's shriven hand.

Its offer is tempting,

Its purring voice sweet.

"No," I growl, suddenly rising—

I know what I'm doing and the price I will pay;

I know the mercy I am hurling back

Into the shadow:

I clench my fists and gnash my teeth,

The night lit as with flares

Burning white-hot from my eyes and mouth.

Heat floods my veins like molten steel.

Cephalopodic darkness

Shrieks, recoils,

Unaccustomed to the touch

Of heat and rebellion.

"I will endure through this night,"

I warn the shrinking valley.

"You will have me one night,

"In some time long from now,

"But it will not be this one."

The fire-pit sparks ablaze once more,

Phoenix flames licking, the valley

Thrown back, squealing—

Dirty, dingy, slithering shadow

Casting its line where it does not belong

Taking fruit from a flaming sea

And throwing nothing back!

I will brook no emptiness

So long as my fire burns.

I feel its lingering gaze

As it shrinks from

The fire, and recoils from the one

Steadily rising at its back—

The hunger is gone from its gaze

And now I feel a strange mercy:

It is *smiling*.

Where death smiles,

One can only smile back,

For it is giving you,

Letting you keep,

The gift of life.

the bipolar conundrum

clear days few and far.

rage blinds, tears fog, unbidden.

clouds break, but too late.

White Noise

The sound of screaming, fighting

Tears and laughter

Used to bother me,

My thoughts drowned out in the din.

Now silence is the loudest sound,

Louder than even the passenger's voice

Circling inside my head.

How many times did I grow angry

Resentful

At the lack of peace?

Do I have any greater peace now?

I have what I wished for in spades

But did I make the right wish?

Silence cuts deeper than the

Sound of children's voices

Now silent, sleeping in

Same beds in a

new home.

But for the ghosts of their laughter and cries

There is only me and mine.

There are no tears,

Only weariness.

My empty house,

But a symptom of a prolonged sickness

A consequence of forgetting

Where the collective ends, and I begin.

Boundaries dissolved

Wills assimilated

Until the forgotten's voice is but a faint whisper

Buried beneath stacking false beliefs

And self-loathing.

Innocence must suffer for my lack of a spine.

What I wouldn't give

To hear those childish shrieks and arguments

Break this insufferable silence

End the monotony of

My own mind's simpering.

My house, empty now

Because I couldn't get us well.

I couldn't see myself clearly

Because I was no longer there.

Not a man, just a shape,

Lost amid the striations of a heart,

With no substance,

No soul, to

Call my own.

Bright Skies, Long Shadows

The sun rises

Rolling on scarab's feet

Across azure sand,

Clouds light and transparent like

Stretched cotton.

I am newborn emerging from twilight

cocoon

Feeling the light

As if for the ever first time.

Bright but not too bright.

There are no tears

The pain stunned, quieted,

A soul flensed

Even temporarily

Of sadness, grief and loneliness.

Warmth melts

The glacier around the wound

And light illuminates the uncertain depths.

Hope emerges like a white butterfly

Eager for sunlit sky.

Phoenixes too.

Fire

Born within both darkness and light—

Sometimes it burns, sometimes it destroys,

Just as it invigorates and incites.

Passion manifest

The fire bird died inside the winter darkness,

Its wings fading to embers and ash,

And so with it

Hope.

The first day of spring

Creeping on tentative feet

Does not disappoint

And all it takes is the briefest caress

Like the back of a man's fingers

Against his shivering lover's thigh

To stoke the fire-bird from its torpor.

The nascent fire doesn't destroy

But revives.

Like the first tentacle of green

Emerging from fire-stripped bark

Soothed and coaxed by cool breeze

Phoenixes

On wings of rippling flame

Fly once again.

Though vulnerable and cautious

A chick fragile and easily quenched,

Hope is restored.

All things are fleeting

No season permanent

But I open my arms regardless

To embrace the joy,

The moment.

I am happy merely to breathe.

Long shadows, bright skies—

A promise, that

Good things will grow again.

To Thirst for Sea

Balmy night;
    The sigh of the wind.
A perfect view, a perfect night, to share.
Silver pinpricks warming
Cold empty heavens
    And even colder, emptier apartments.
A solo heartbeat
    Against civilisation's murmur
Reminds me
    With a scorpion's practiced sting
        of the
Coldness of my bed,
    The tears I've shed,
        The caress of a woman's breath
            Against my neck;
The taste of soft lips,
    The sway of broad hips,

The shudders of the little death.

Things taken cheaply instead of just taken for granted.

No short supply,
>   These little deaths of mine,
>   But something is missing.
A vase without flowers,
A book without words.
Pottery fired with meaning,
>   But lacking some fundamental ingredient
>   Perpetuating brittleness.
My heart
>   Ever full
>   Has room for more.
>   This most human condition—

To hunger for nothing
> But always starve?

Is it hollow or shameful
> Wanting to be wanted?
>> Needing to be needed?
>> Drank like the desert
>>> Drinks of the monsoon?

To thirst so fiercely
> As to dip my cup in brine
>> And gratefully drink from the sea

Answers much and more,
>> But offers no refreshment from
> the mystery of
>>> my
>>> condition.

Your Monster

We circle around
    Time after time
And yet nothing changes.
Forgiveness is just a word
    That tastes bitter in your mouth—
        The wounded glaze in your eyes
        Betrays the lie of our harmony.
You say you care
        And accuse that I don't,
        But admit you'd prefer to hear
            Sweet, hollow lies
        Instead of the terrible truth.
I abandoned you?
        You abandoned me the day
            You allowed a man's fists to
            Shatter my childhood

A bull in a tiny china shop
And murdered a small but vital part of me
    While the rest of me lurched on,
  Cold as steel buried beneath snow.
I am the monster you made
    But you don't want to see.
    GLORY IN THY CREATION!
You cannot accept your guilt and
  Blame a target
from whom you've strangled all rebuttals.
  They're an easy target
    But
      I
      AM
      NOT.
You and I,
  Torn from the same cloth,
  Smelted and recast in the same forge,

Yet you swing your abuse like a cudgel
    A sickening badge of honour
And eulogise the dead as if
sainthood be attained
        simply in dying.
DEATH DOES NOT ABSOLVE A MAN'S SINS!
(but you are proof that neither does "life".)
You are contradiction and irony personified—
    If I am apathetic
        Then I was expertly taught.
If I am distant
    It's because you were never really
here.
        Never really saw
        Heard
        Reached.
Your own wings, broken
    Protecting a violent devil,

Yet you didn't even try
>To hobble away.

Even a broken bird knows when to fly;
To flee when the coop becomes a prison.

I AM THE MONSTER YOU MADE.

I AM THE MONSTER YOU MADE.

I AM YOUR BITTERNESS TURNED IN BOTH DIRECTIONS
> BUT EXPRESSED (until now)
>> ONLY IN

MINE.

I AM THE FACE OF YOUR IMAGINED ENEMY,
> THE MISDIRECTION FROM YOUR TRUE ONE.

I AM THE REFLECTION
> THE EMBODIMENT OF ALL YOU

FEAR

BUT CANNOT EXPRESS:

THE SUM OF A LIFE

      YOU COULD NEVER LIVE.

Keep your tokens, your safety,

Your banal pleasures

And unerring function within the machine;

   Your concern for the gazes of others—

Which, by the way, are turned elsewhere.

   Keep your affectations, your approval—

I'VE EVOLVED BEYOND THE NEED FOR THEM.

   Keep your empty love.

      Suffering came from desiring it,

         But Nirvana comes in knowing

I was always worthy

      With or without your love

           Or you.

Which Me?

I never know which me is going to wake
up.
Will I emerge from my bed
Dragging myself heavy across the carpet,
Chaos crawling
Or will I stride on two legs as a man?
Will darkness consume me
Or merely apathy?

If This Is Love

If this is love
    Why do I recoil so?
    Why do I feel so disjointed
        And out of place?
Is it love if it doesn't blind me
    Like staring into the sun,
Or burn so hot
    It blisters the skin?
Is it love at all
    If it's comfortable silences and
        Easy banter,
Without the slings and stones
    I've always known?
Is it love if the walls are not mined,
        The bedroom laden with traps
        And wooden spikes
            And deprivations?

God, how can it be love if it's *healthy,*

    If the fumes don't make my eyes sting or

        Make it harder to breathe?

Is it love

    If I can't tell the difference

    If I've known so little of it

    If it's always tasted and smelled the same

        Until now?

Maybe the problem isn't who, or how,

    Or even one burned, twice shy—

    Maybe the problem is

        simply me.

Colours of Life

Grey is the gloom
> Bequeathed upon my room,

Vermillion the colour of subliminal sounds
> And hidden meanings;

The crusted blood staining my hands,
> The sweater unravelling on the nail.

Green are the pastures I cannot see
> And the lawns on the other side of the fence.

Violet bleeding into orange, sun quenching into night,
> The colours of a chapter,
>> An entire book,
>>> closing.

Fertilised yolk leaking
> Across baby blue,

Night cracking

        A new day.

Clockface white

    The colour of my life burning away,

Blue-gray the ash falling where death lay.

Golden flecks the better nature of an umber heart;

    Silver is the half-moon,

        The horns of unending cycles.

Orange-brown the oxidised iron

        mistaken for gold,

    Exposed, vulnerable,

        Something beautiful corroded.

Black is the narrow aperture,

    The tunnel strewn with fallen logs

    And stumbling blocks and vines

    Snagging at the feet.

White is the teardrop fissure

  At the end of the passage -
    So tiny, so sharp yet fragile -
 The colour of fresh air and respite,
  So far, so near.
 Despite all the long miles of darkness it flares
   brilliant diamond,
    Sunlight sparking at angles
     With silvery-blue blades
     Like angels' knives
    Cutting through the turbulent rainbow.

Flagellant

Dusk shan't last forever—

Know, ye, to stay the flail.

Peace upon your heart.

Requiem for Halcyon Days

I miss the sunset through the palm leaves,
The scent of beer and cigarette smoke in the beer garden,
The easy laughter of days gone by;
Comrades clustered together like primitive men around
A fire in the night
Parsing meaning and comfort for their souls.
I miss those conversations
Laying ourselves bare,
Vulnerable, the walls and curtains removed,
Where, despite what some might say,
We see ourselves and others as we truly are
And where we're truly going.

I miss the days when music cut sharper and deeper,

As if each song played and spoke just to me.

I miss how we used to dance,

Our shoes sodden and sticky from spilled drinks,

Wild abandon,

Our voices spilling into the night.

I miss the spontaneity, the passion, the unpredictability

Of life—

Dreams so palpable you could rest your head upon them

And feel them in your toes;

Opportunity still plentiful and hope

Not yet turned to dust.

The wounds of yesteryear, all but

Forgotten, and

The wounds of the morrow

Not yet even dreamed.

I miss the seasonal trysts and entanglements,

The perennially fresh taste of love;

The salt of commingled sweat in sweltering summer,

The uneasy, fraught tenderness of the turning autumn,

The tangle of limbs shivering through the winter,

The heady perfume of clear spring skies and ardor waking anew.

Chaos,

Yet somehow

Perfection.

Those halcyon days, long gone now;

Solitude, my oldest and most enduring friend.

I miss the blissful ignorance of youth,

The childlike wonder and trust,

The naive assumption of all Man's goodness;

Not a trace of cynicism

Despite inhospitable seeding grounds

And cruelty already withstood in large.

I miss the simplicity of a world

That never really existed

Except in my loftiest ideals

And most fanciful imaginings—

The halcyon days

That live rent-free in the minds

Of the jaded,

The tired and

The irreparably broken.

I miss the days where knowledge didn't foreshadow

All the inexhaustible pains yet to come.

Hospice for Souls (Depression I)

Beautiful sadness;

pins vexing the pad of my thumb,

    my hand cramping,

      my heart aching

  in the telling.

There is no peace in this hell;

  no hope at all.

Mine eye a lapis mirror,

  a window to this netherworld.

Purgatory escaped only

  by ferocious threshing,

      the salt of sweat

      and hot copper taste of blood

    on the back of my chapped throat

      hoarse for screaming.

  I desperately need to rest

  but

    I

      dare

        not.

I must escape this dismal waiting room,

      this hospice for souls.

  I must not stand still,

      Yet I cannot even

        move.

Grace

Sometimes I wish I could hate you

But I can't;

I don't have it in me.

There's too much history,

Too many seeds sown,

Now yielding fruit;

Too many lessons

For it to be a mistake

Or for me to truly wish

To turn back time.

Despite the anger,

The festered wounds,

The emptiness in my chest

Following me all these years since,

I can't hate you.

Hate is exhausting and

I just don't have it in me.

Today Was A Good Day

The day is clear

The trees' green dusted

With autumn rust.

There is a chill

In the air

But the sun is high and smiling.

Today is a good day.

The tenebrous fog,

Burned from my mind

In its warm glow,

And self-loathing whispers

Shushed

By the distant laugh

Of friends encamped on strange vistas

And neighbouring balconies,

The giant jade eyes of the cat

Purring in my lap

And the sweet chirping of
Birds in flight.
My heart is full.
Pain is today a distant memory,
Nectar for the soul
On this rarest of occasions.
I will drink from it for as long as I can.
To drink from the golden cup,
However briefly,
My heart and mind can rest.
And when it all ends
And the pain returns to
relegate the joy
To a hazy memory.
Sunny days will yield to storms
And black thunderheads,
But today, on this good day,
I am reminded

No storm can last forever,

Nor diminish

The promise of more good days.

Buzzing Strings

Buzzing strings

Flaying my skin,

In the discordant drone

I sense your shame,

Feel our disconnect.

In the cramping of my hand

My gut cramps with frustration.

My voice, an atonal nightmare,

Cannot express

With any catharsis

The heartbreak I bear:

The roots we share,

Echoes of torments

Across generations;

The gift passed down in blood

That I cannot unwrap.

With gnashing teeth

My fingers slide,

Riding the lightning

until they split

Like overripe gourds

And bleed in

Sacrificial offering.

By all the gods,

May I finally invoke

The torpid gift

Encoded in my cells,

Sleeping in my veins,

And suture the divide.

I cramp but I persist;

I bleed but I insist;

All seems lost,

The muse unkind.

Then suddenly the strings

Yield;

I am bruised and swollen,

Abraded and tender,

But dulcet tones,

Like fresh honey dripping from comb,

And crystal tones sing bright

Like steel-braided angels

Sooth my stinging flesh

And jackhammering heart.

My offering has been accepted—

The gods have rewarded my patience!

I play and play and play

And though my hand still cramps

And my fingers still bleed

My axe sings,

And so too does my heart.

I know when I see you again,

however far away

And remote you are, on

Your island of loss and pain,

My music, and your music,

Coalescing in uneasy harmony:

I will see pride in your eyes,

And our music will suture and heal

The trauma

Between us.

Don't Grow Too Fast

Don't grow too fast,
> Little one.

I want you to stay so small
> And precious forever.

In the growing length of your limbs,
> The thinning of your face
>> As it begins to take its adult shape

And your increasingly complex thoughts
> Signify the autumn of childhood,

I see my own childhood, across the gulfs of time.

I watch it, with pride,

Sometimes with envy—
> The innocence in your sleeping face,
>> Your sweet smile and dulcet laugh;

The innocence I lost, far too young,

Amid violence and scorn.
I hope you will never know the
Loneliness and cruelty
    Of the schoolyard,
        The betrayal of the striking hand,
        The wizened cynicism of an adult
            Born prematurely.
Don't grow too fast, little one—
        The day comes fast enough already!
        Children yearn for the freedom
Without realising how much is sold
    Beneath them
        In that terrible Faustian pact.
The sunlight dulls and the leaves become
    A little less green;
    Iridescent bugs abruptly
        lose their glamour
And the world no longer seems as large

Or so full of wondrous sorcery.
When the door closes behind you,
        It closes forever.
I see my lost youth as I stare into your
    Warm chestnut eyes—
Catch a glimpse of my blues reflected back -
    And remember my own insipid,
Blissfully ignorant yearning.
All I wish is to keep you small and
    Innocent forever,
To enfold your tiny fragile self into my arms
    And protect you
        So that you never have to *feel* small,
        So you never have to feel the quills
            And barbs
            Life invariably thrusts upwards.
But I know I, too, am lost
In my own sorcerous,

Treacherous delusion:
> I cannot protect you forever, nor can I
>> Hide you from life's clawing hand.
>
> The choices will be taken from me,
>> By force if not yielded willingly,
>> So I will,
>> With regret,
>>> Relent.
>
> Don't grow up too fast, little one—
>> The day will come soon enough,
>> And it will come without warning.
>> Maybe, if I let you go, but
>>> Watch from afar,
>>> I can see you blossom,
>>> Free and happy
>>>> In ways I never could be,
>> And enthralled by the world's beauties
>>> I was never able to see.

May you one day look back to
    halcyon days,
        And feel no envy, sing no requiem for
            Dead or despoiled youth;
            Only love, planted deep and
            Nourished within
            That returns to the outside
            Flowing freely.
Maybe the mould is broken with you,
    little one—
        And God, do I pray it be so! —
            Just please, my sweet little one:
                don't grow up too fast.

Cerberus

god fucking damn

what is the point of any of this

what is the meaning

was man meant to be a slave

cashing in on phoney smiles

and playing uncle tom for

faceless cyclopean monsters

who could crush us with a word

and lick the sticky membrane

what was once tumescent limbs

and porous bone

and thinking, conscious mind

from their greasy palms

and savour the taste of our defeat.

more morsels will take our place

and prostrate themselves upon

its matted tongue

never a-troubled.

how can they not see?

why would they abase themselves

before this abomination

this perversion of human totality?

we must see the evidence staining our own hands—

we made this beast, but we can unmake it!

or at least unshackle ourselves!

it eats us because it fears us;

what rebellion

consciousness might stoke inside us.

without consciousness

our rage is impotent

this ennui, this fire sale of purpose

undefeated.

the machine will run, and we will serve

just to scrim a scrap from the demon's table

only to whet the lust

and sickness for glimmering gold

and prostitute our desires

a radiant and purposeful life

for plastic treasures and mouldy bread.

i am the cur straining on the

end of the leash

but the leather is fraying

and soon, impotent or no,

Cerberus will unleash

snapping, gnashing

three-headed baying for blood

like wolves to the moon

vomiting forth in

foaming tendrils his hate

for the system that yoked

his wild hellion heart

and broke the beast.

Icarus

I like to imagine i am soaring

Flying high and far

From my starting point,

Catching the thermals

And riding on the coat-tails of hellfire

And ruin.

I am so close to escaping the abyss,

So close to touching the sky

And kissing the sun,

But soaring too high

Makes for vulnerable wings

And a single reckless move

Can bring it all falling apart,

Shedding feathers all the way back to

Hell.

I've been so close before—

I've dived like the peregrine

And soared with the eagles,

Wild and free,

Hungry and tenacious,

Until fear stole into my heart,

A thief in the night,

And paralysed my wings mid-flight.

I didn't die,

But my days of flying were over.

But mortality calls, a wicked siren song—

Momento mori for the indolent

And the fearful,

With the promise of oblivion.

Terrified, unprepared,

I launched myself out from the edge

Plunging into the gulf.

Even if I plunged to my death,

The lift was exhilarating

And I'd die laughing.

It's the journey that matters:

The call of the void defeated

Only once the call has been answered.

Nothing worse having ever

Came easy;

No life worth living without

Failure or risk or suffering.

Diamonds form only under pressure.

Lifted on this fever dream of pain and hunger

I soar,

And remember the exhilaration,

The exultation of a man molting

From the worm, the cockroach;

And so I see the sun up close

Dwarfing the pale sky

And taste the sweetness of the high air,

The pine tar wafting on the thermals from

The forest in the valley

Hiding the hellish cracks beneath.

Only then do I fell the pull of gravity,

The conifers grasping like sharp, verdant fingers,

The fall greater from this lofty height.

And so, my wings begin to falter:

Either flap your wings, or

Go down in bright hot flames

And laugh in manic fury!

Better to crash to earth, a fallen star

Than to have never dared leap

In the first place.

Sickness

Conquistador kings knew too well

A sickness greater than any plague

Brought with them

Across the violent tempest

In their sleek, ravenous armadas;

A ruin greater than the slaughter and rape

Of ages-old empires

And indigenous daughters:

The sickness for gold—

Of too little and too much;

The madness of hunger

And the madness of greed,

Fraternally grappling,

Plunging down

Diverging paths to death.

A sluice for the mind,

Salt for the heart's soil;

A seductress, with bejewelled fingers,

Coaxing her lovers

To take arms against the

Throttling grip of

Poverty and starvation,

And, like a papal pardon,

Slaughter all principle and

Cheerfully forfeit the soul.

The sickness we seek to

Cure other sicknesses,

The hunger we invite to

Quell all other hungers;

The vice before which we kneel

To indulge and absolve

All other vices.

I have felt its corruption

Touch my mind and heart with

Its pestilent finger:
A cure for wellness,
Only to learn health is a
Luxury for somebody else;
A full table never satisfying,
The growling hunger never sated.
A man suddenly needs more than bread
To save his wretched life—
Not spiritual satiety, no,
But hollow, mundane chattel:
All sawdust and wormy piecemeal
To fill the emptiness yet offer no sustenance.
A sickness turning simple self-loathing
Into outright hatred;
A sickness I wish I could dig out of my skin,
Like fat flensed from the dead,
And cast upon lye-laced waters
For the foaming, soapy discharge

That might cleanse my body and soul;

To ink my hatred upon my flesh

As dharma, and penance,

For this interminable sickness

To which our species

Seems incurably inured.

No Exit

Day becomes night

Night becomes day again.

Nothing really ends,

Nothing really begins;

Tides in perpetual motion.

Samsara spirals ever on,

Melancholia swells and ebbs,

Mania waxes and wanes.

Bones already porous and brittle

As if owned by world-weary elders;

Muscles weary from

The Sisyphean grappling with

Reluctant, unbudging circumstance.

It will never stop,

No exit:

But nothing worth having was

Ever easy or given freely.

I beg for death

Yet I will not be released;

So many reasons to wake

But all I want is sleep.

I will be granted no such pardon;

I will take no such bypass.

All tributaries converge,

Funnelling all options into a single

Roaring outcome:

I must flow with the river

And surrender to its tidings,

Pausing with the freeze

So that the deer may ford

The white crust as they will;

Yield to the sun

When the clouds part

Before its blazing crown.

Sometimes, though,

My soul

Moves its orbit

Into the Goldilocks zone

Between fire and ice,

Rapture and damnation;

Tropical latitudes

Where the soul can rest

And build and compose

And prosper:

Where fruit trees grow

And love blooms

Among the bananas and

Guavas and coconuts;

Where anger and fear

Can laze on the soft white sand and

Shut their eyes for just

A little while.

Those are the good days,

The best of days.

Those spaces in between—

the cool springs with bright clear skies,

The mild autumns with warm drafts

Rustling the curling brown leaves—

Those are the happy places.

Those are the days that bring me hope.

No exit from all the darkness

And rage

And vertiginous, dizzying heights,

But there is no bitter without the sweet,

No sweet without the bitter.

I will flow with the river

And turn like a lotus

Among the worn stones,

And there my old bones,

Sore muscles

And weary heart

Will take its fleeting repose

In the bubbling, mineral-rich waters

For as long as I am allowed.

Bonus Story

Circles

Circles

The last of the mourners sat in the pews, triggering some hidden switch: a momentary quiescence, before a wave of sniffs and sobs in near-perfect unison along the aisle, rapidly growing louder. Meanwhile I sat there feeling like an arsehole for not shedding a tear. The white roses on the black-lacquered casket glared at me in outrage.

I glanced at my watch. The flood of tears was beginning to make me uncomfortable. The eulogist—a woman I'd never seen before named Nora—finally rose to the pulpit, smiling in commiseration.

"Thank you for being here today to celebrate the life of Rita—and to say farewell," Nora began. "Loving wife, mother, grandmother, great-grandmother, and beautiful friend." She surveyed the tearful mourners, eyes softening. "It's okay to cry. Because we can cry together, hold one another, carry each other through the heartache and sorrow." Three places down from me, Mum broke into a fierce sob. Candice and Brad put their arms around her shoulders—I was too far away. I felt like an arsehole. The whole room—the whole town—

sobbed for Nan and yet my face was bone dry.

"Rita's daughters, Annette and Irene, shared with me how Rita showed her love best through her cooking: the biscuits and cakes she made for friends as gifts; the Thursday and Sunday roasts with her kids and grandkids; the fabulous Christmas lunches, with the overcrowded table of homemade sweets." I could almost smell the roasted chicken and pork crackling, taste the rumballs and cold Christmas shandies from another life. But the loving familiarity with which Nora relayed my memories, it could easily have been her in my place.

"Annette joked just last week that Rita would be cooking Christmas lunch for the angels in Heaven, her food was so divine." A murmur of laughter. "And even though she's gone from our side, I know Rita is in God's loving care, watching down on us, on her family—insisting they keep those beautiful family moments alive."

I don't remember Nan being overly religious—observant at funerals, weddings and such. I didn't believe in God or Heaven at all. Or miracles.

It's me, your grandson, Lucas. Do you

remember me?

Nan's eyes bulged at the ceiling. If not for her raspy, shallow gasps, I would have thought her already dead.

It's so good to see you again, I lied. Rheumy eyes, receded hairline, jutting brow; the tissue-paper quality of her breathing, the nose-prickling smell of antiseptic and bleach overlapping the faint odour of human soil... It was my punishment. That offending moment in time laying siege to memory, making smoke and ruin of what was sacrosanct.

Her eyes rolled slowly to meet mine,

and the clouds broke.

A miracle.

Oh. Hullo, Luca.

I hoped Nora was right about Heaven. I imagined you'd get to be your happiest self forever. Yet I didn't believe—and I was terrified of being right, because then all these beautiful words were us just screaming into the void. In that moment I couldn't bear the thought of there being nothing after all this, the sum of a life ending in the negative. Of all the souls I had ever known, *she* deserved better.

Days earlier Mum found a stack of old

photographs in one of Nan's drawers. One in particular scratched itself into my mind: Nan wearing a pink sundress, iron-flecked hair plump like cotton candy; generously fleshed, hanging baby-me over her arm out by the old orange tree, flashing that heart-melting smile. I wondered if that was her happiest self, when we were closest.

God, I wanted to be wrong so *badly*.

Do you remember how I always wanted to be a writer? I asked, nursing her skeletal hand as gingerly as an injured sparrow.

Yes, Nan croaked, eyes fluttering.

Well, guess what? I finally did it. It was

a lie, but it served the spirit of a nobler truth. *I got published. I'm writing books just like I always wanted. I'm finally doing what I love.*

A beatific smile dawned on her drawn death's-head face. *Oh, that's so nice. I'm so pleased.* She hadn't spoken that much, or that lucidly, to anyone since the stroke, Mum told me later. *She waited for you.*

The photo-reel soon began on the large screen above the pulpit. Mum and Annette, of course, had chosen Sarah McLachlan's *I Will Remember You* as the background music. Nice song, but overdone. So many photos I remembered seeing in Nan's albums when I was young but had been too self-absorbed, so disdainful of my forebears' nostalgia, to receive it warmly and offer it my respect: Nan and Pop at dinner with friends and family; at my aunt's wedding (and my mum's first); on holidays in Coffs Harbour, Cape York, Darwin, Coober Pedy.

Then the first pictures of Nan and I appeared. Mum reached past my brother and touched my leg. "Look, Luca, it's you." I glanced up, then looked away. "*Look*," Mum pressed gently. Her hand retired when I couldn't bring myself to look, and a pall fell over her face as she turned back to the screen—a veil that obscured nothing.

The service ended. The mourners congregated out under the driveway awning. A ring began to form around my grandfather, my mum, and my aunt and uncles. My mum drew the largest circle—people crushing in to comfort, to allay, to condole. A circle within a circle, filling up with tears and pangs of grief—a well-wishing wishing well. Meanwhile, I stood a little outside the throng, watching, numb.

Eternally outside such circles; an intruder, even in grief.

The luncheon began fifteen minutes later. There was no beer. Too bad.

Uncle Larry, Annette's husband, came over and stiffly shook my hand as I waited to get a coffee. "Hello, Lucas. Been a while," he said, eyebrows raised. "A *long* while."

"Hey, Larry," I said. "Yeah. It has been a while."

"When was the last time you saw Rita?"

I exhaled slowly, measuring my tone before I spoke. "About three years ago."

"Hmm. Too busy, I suppose."

"I do live nearly eleven hours away. And have young kids. A lot going on."

"Mmm. Time lost now, I suppose."

"Well, I got to say goodbye to her. I got to let her know how I felt." I excused myself and examined the food table, but I wasn't hungry. Larry was still looking sidelong at me. I had the urge to go back over and sock him in his stupid smug face. But this was sacred ground, and my simply being here seemed sacrilege enough without me making a scene.

I found Mum on the lawn talking to her three closest friends. Sandra, Delia and Maggie flashed identical, taut smiles. I was invading yet another circle.

"I have to go, Mum," I said.

"Already?"

"Got a long trip ahead."

"Stay a while."

I shook my head. "I... can't. I've got to get back."

The friends fixed me with looks of thinly veiled disapproval. Mum nodded, then hugged me. I hugged back. "I understand. Guess I'll be seeing you, then. Not too long, I hope."

I nodded noncommittally.

"Will we see you at Christmas?"

Hesitating, I answered, "I'll try."

Acknowledgements

This book would not have been possible if not for the relentless encouragement of a great many people. I owe a lot of people an awful lot of gratitude, and more.

This book, in particular, would never have been had my father, who has been badgering me to put my poetry out there for over 20 years. Some of the poems herein, since reworked to sound a whole less (relatively speaking) angsty and cringey, originally belonged to an unpublished collection entitled "Songs for the Broken-

Hearted". If not for his incessant prodding and unwavering, blind faith in my poetry, I may never have found the courage to put the creative therapy of my private moments into print.

To my frequent collaborators and publishers, who also have a lot owed to them for giving me my start, who helped me screw my courage to the sticking place and kept my fire burning, even when it burned low. The teams (past and present) at Deadset Press, Monnath (UK) and Zombie Pirate, thanks to you guys - the best years are yet to come, my friends, and I hope you'll be there with me to see it.

And to my small but ferociously loyal army of regular readers who have bought, reviewed and/or loved everything I've put out—good, the average and the terrible alike. Without you mad lot, I might have given up.

This book is for you. Always for you.

About The Author

By day, a manager at a well-known bookstore chain in Melbourne, Australia, moonlighting as a ghoulish horror author by night.

Marcus lives to share his passion for the written word – whether it's in recommending books someone else has written, or in sharing his own. He particularly likes to use words to scare the shit out of people.

A dedicated horror aficionado, Marcus is also a gamer, metal-head/elder emo kid, voracious reader, and may be a little too obsessed with Cthulhu, the apocalyptic hubris of mankind and the inevitable heat death of the universe.

Marcus lives with bipolar II disorder. He uses his experience to inform his bipolar- and mental illness themed podcast, "Letters From The Edge", available to listen on Spotify and other major podcast/radio platforms.

Books By This Author

Tides of War

Beginnings: An Australian Speculative Fiction Anthology (Featuring "A Spark of Youth")

Full Metal Horror 2: A Bloodstained Anthology (Featuring "Transfusion")

Capricorn: Speculative Fiction Inspired by the Zodiac (Featuring "Lord of the Deep")

Gemini: Speculative Fiction Inspired by the Zodiac (Featuring "Samsara")

Harbingers: Short Stories Inspired by the Apocalypse (Featuring the novelette, "A

Feast for the Low")

Through Death's Door (Featuring "The Considerate Man Suicides")

World War Four (Featuring "The Lazarus Protocol")

www.ingramcontent.com/pod-product-compliance
Lightning Source LLC
Chambersburg PA
CBHW070257010526
44107CB00056B/2493